life: or something like it

life:
or something
like it

Catherine Sharpe-Lewis

POETRY CHAPEL
PRESS

Copyright © 2023 Catherine Sharpe-Lewis

All rights reserved. No part of this publication may be reproduced, distributed, or transmitted in any form or by any means, without prior written permission of the author.

The moral rights of the author have been asserted.

Author website: www.catherinesharpe-lewis.com
Author email: hello@catherinesharpe-lewis.com

Poetry Chapel Press
Sunshine Coast, QLD, Australia

Cover Illustration: Copyright © 2023 Catherine Sharpe-Lewis

Edited: Rachel Huckel
                 www.rachelhuckel.com

Also available in eBook format.
ISBN: 978-0-6458086-1-2

life: or something like it / Catherine Sharpe-Lewis. -- 1st ed.
ISBN: 978-0-6458086-0-5

Dedicated to my father, who called me a poet, and life an adventure.

And to my Mum, who embodies both courage and compassion.

Table of Contents

Introduction	1
A Note on How This Book Works	6
life: definition	7
Part One: Entering the Storm	8
Rest	10
The Life Well Travelled	12
Beautiful Monster	14
Crave	15
This is War	16
Dirt	17
The Gatherers	19
The Ache	20
Evening Debates	21
Shadows	22
The Beautiful Storm	23
Single Mum Guilt	24
I Wish I Were A Puppy	26
The Drifter	28
earth after rain	29
Time Goes Dripping By	30
Messy and Bright	32

Table of Contents

Part Two: The Eye of the Storm   33

Daughter of Eve	35
Brain Fog	36
Broken	37
The Herald	38
Remember This Moment	39
Jeff (Until We Meet Again)	40
Balloon	42
The Machine	44
Do Not Get Drunk	46
For Ed.	48
I Am His Moon	49
A Poem for a Mother on her Birthday	50
Mall Thoughts	52
In the Moment	54
Winds of Change	55
Pink Bedsheets	56

Table of Contents

Part Three: Coming Out of the Storm   58

The Thing I Admire Most	60
Warrior	63
Prayer of a Broken Vessel	64
Love Allows the Journey	65
Freedom Dance	66
A Weekend Blessing	67
A Closer Look	68
The Wings of Forgiveness	70
She Shall	72
After glow	73
Happy?	74
Home	76
Gift-Wrapped	78
God's Poem	79
Rest	81
Acknowledgements	84
References	86

Introduction

Life is hard. There is simply no way around it. If you live long enough, you will experience heartache. People fail us. Circumstances fail us. Disappointments abound. When I was younger, someone told me that you are always in one of three stages of life. You are either entering a storm, in the midst of a storm, or coming out of a storm. At the time, this statement struck me as particularly macabre. Who wants to believe that life is like *that*? How depressing! It took another six years for me to understand the deep truth of the adage. My childhood was *amazing*. I grew up in paradise. I had a stable, nuclei family. I lived on a property that was literally designed to introduce high-end city kids to the delights of the country (complete with pet kangaroos, indoor rock-climbing, and river-front access with canoes). I lived on the same property as my best friend. I loved school. I was smart, I had friends, I had freedom, dreams, and prospects.

Then age sixteen hit. The start of complex and unrecognised mental ill-health reared its head – anxiety, compliments of mum's genes, severe depression, compliments of dad's. I gave my heart to a toxic relationship. I didn't achieve my dreams by eighteen, and somehow interpreted that as failure. Things that were previously clear cut started to blur.

At twenty-five years old, as a young wife and mum, the entire house of cards fell over. I experienced betrayal and extreme disappointment. People I thought I could trust let me down. It. Was. HARD.

Since that time, life has continued to be an undulation of high exultation, stability of sorts, and extreme nose dives. At best, life is stable. At worst…

Something that has struck me deeply has been the realisation that my story is not unique. Being a white, female, upper-middle class Australian citizen did not protect me from pain. My deep faith in God did not shelter me from heartache, or from bad things happening which were outside of my control. Saying "no" to drugs and alcohol didn't prevent serious mental ill-health from materialising in my life. It *just happened anyway.*

Oddly enough, two books I normally wouldn't have touched shed some serious revelation on these experiences. The first was a book about the faith of her late majesty, Queen Elizabeth II (Delffs, 2019). When her majesty died in September 2022, I was really struck by the circumstances surrounding her life. She was an amazing woman. The longest reining British monarch, unexpectedly rising to world power at only twenty-five years old, Queen Elizabeth saw ten decades, two centuries and a new millennium (Roberts, 2022). She was the most famous woman in the world. When she died, her ducks were not all in a row. Wars continued – some freshly developed. Relationships were troublesome. Wonderful things, and hard things, continued to exist. I have spent a lifetime *not* paying attention to the Royal family. But as Queen Elizabeth's reign was coming to an end, I became intrigued with how someone who had subconsciously been a part of my life for my whole life could do so in such a way that she could *be* there, like a familiar piece of beloved furniture, and still *stand firm*, without making a fuss. Like the rest of the world, I was vaguely aware of the general upheaval and unrest plaguing the Royal family. After reading Prince Harry's memoir, *Spare* (2023), I was heartbroken over it. Even the most respected and famous of humans, rich beyond comprehension, seemingly above the law...*even they* struggle. With *life*. Because life is hard. No matter who you are.

And yet...

Life is also beautiful.
And not in a superficial way. The beauty that flashes around us and inside us is not a mere band-aid on the mortal wound of life. Beauty is

the antidote to pain. In the Christian faith, the concept of beauty can be interpreted as *grace*. Life has a gentle grace to it that takes away the breath of the attentive. Those who look for beauty, find it. It doesn't appear *in place of* pain and heart-ache: it exists *despite* it.

The storm I am currently in is the hardest one I've dealt with yet. I am currently cut off from the people I care about most in this world, without any framework or timetable for when or how I might get back to them. The injustice of my position has me beating my breast in grief and sorrow, anger and anguish. It is really, really hard. And yet.

And yet. The most unexpected of people have my back. Those who have known far greater heartache than I have welcomed me into their worlds. The gift of words is allowing me to communicate in spirit, and I am trusting, is building a sacred manuscript which my people will one day be able to read and know that they were not forgotten by the one who loves them.

Flowers continue to blossom in rocky places. Building and maintaining physical gardens is teaching me life-lessons in the metaphysical. I am learning to embrace the discomfit of cold air.

If life is a storm, then Vivian Greene was right: "Life isn't about waiting for the storm to pass, it's about learning how to dance in the rain."

I hope this book helps you to find the grace in the storms. Life is hard. But life is beautiful.

Be blessed, friends.

      Catherine Sharpe-Lewis.

A Note on how this book works

This collection doesn't follow traditional 'categories', given that life as a rule is not neat and tidy. However, I have assigned one of four symbols to each poem, so the reader can broadly identify what 'part' of life may be found within any given one. These symbols are found in the top corner of each new poem.

 Moments: Poems capturing innocent or suspended moments in time.

 The Struggle: Poems addressing hard subjects and emotions. May contain potential triggers.

 Hope in Struggle: Poems acknowledging good things inside of hard subjects.

 Faith Poems: Poems that bring God into the story.

life:
/lʌɪf/

noun
1. 1. the condition that <u>distinguishes</u> people, animals and plants from <u>inorganic</u> matter, including the capacity for growth, reproduction, functional activity, and <u>continual</u> change preceding death.

(The Oxford English Dictionary, 2023)

Part One: Entering the Storm

Storms are a majestic phenomenon. If you have ever witnessed a violent storm, you know how breath-taking they can be. Wild and loud, dark, and dramatic; these forces are capable of serious devastation. They make us pause and tremble with fear and awe.

Of course, a storm is far more majestic, and less terror-inducing when you are inside, dry, warm, and protected. Should you have the misfortune to find yourself outside, or caught on a ship, or in a cyclone...entering a storm is *terrifying*.

The storms of life are no exception. When life takes you down unexpectedly, what might seem short-lived and trivial to a bystander can have devastating effects to the participant. It is similar to being caught in the rough ocean. If you have ever been dumped by a wave in the sea, you can appreciate the comparison. When life takes you down unexpectedly, it is hard to breathe. In some instances, taking a breath isn't even an option, for fear of drowning. It is disorienting: You don't know which way is up, and there is no sense of when you might be free to breathe again. You dare not let your breath out in case you can't take another. It is a desperate feeling.

The hard parts of life are no different. The sense of terror is no less real. Even if the danger is minimal, it feels like you won't make it. The hardest part is knowing that all you can do is hold on. Because the only way out is *through*.

Rest

Rest
Is not a dirty word,
Though it is a hard one.
It is hard to
Be still
Long enough to let
The dirt dry and flake
From your
Weary soul.
It is hard to
Unstrap the fetters of the world
And place them at His feet,
Where we were never supposed to pick them up
But did.
Rest requires surrender
Of the control we

Never

Really

Had.

To accept the roll of that
Massive wave looming
In order to find the Deep places
Beyond.
To be still long enough to hear
The selah in the psalm.
To HEAR it,
And to listen
And to KNOW.

Be Still.

Be STILL.

Be still.

Life is waiting there for you.

The Life Well Travelled
                (After Robert Frost)

Two souls diverged in a fractious life
And I,
Confused by the path that had paved my way,
I stood and looked as far as I could,
Found myself in the past with a critical eye.
Egg shells strewn, word bombs exploded,
Weapons I hadn't recognised as loaded
Criss-crossed our paths with their paper cuts,
Lemon juice, vinegar and other vices,
And I,
I discovered I had used these devices!

And both souls that morning equally lay,
Unmarred by events that might
Tar them black:
Is there hope for another day,
Even though there is no going back?
I shall be telling this with a sigh,
Somewhere in the days and years forthwith,
Two souls diverged in a fractious life,
And I –
I forged a path to travel by:
I pray that it might be kindly.

Beautiful Monster

The black dog of Depression
has been worrying my heels,
stealing my sleep, my hope, my energy.
I'm so tired of living
One step behind,
Of hurting
Others…

It keeps bringing me back
To the roaring lie
That I am a monster,
Exotic, exquisite, extraordinary…

Best kept in a cage.

So I cage myself.
Reassemble the bars of defeat
Over my eyelids
To remind myself
That there is no freedom
For an animal
As beautiful
As me.

Crave

I have cigarette cravings for life:

At random intervals throughout the day, I am
Overwhelmed by the insatiable

desire to Live.

I long for it with my entire being,
it clouds my thoughts, my mind.

I gasp for it, even as it racks my body
with fits and tremors,

it calls to me:

    "Come, suck on the marrow of life!"

Then I exhale.

And life on earth goes on.

This Is War

Forgive me Father for the aggression
Underlying my
Craving to live,
to know,
to feel.

You of all people should understand my
Obsession with living
Undermined by my need to Die.

Soul being sucked dry,
Attacked by
Truth diverted
And sincere people sincerely wrong.
Need I say more? This is war.

Dirt

Am I a mop that
you wipe the floor with my soul?
Diluting the arrogance of your caste
in the bucket of my mind,
Stretching me thin to cleanse
the guilty blood
that threatens to stain your
yellow-brick road of perfect?

Do you compress the threads of my dignity
so that your dirty secrets can trickle unseen
into the dark waters?
Tossed out the back
to be mopped up by the dirt and weeds
of your hidden life where
no-one sees and no-one cares?

Don't you know that blood cries out
from the ground and Somewhere
we are seen?
You will be found out.
And we will.
Be.
Found.

The Gatherers
        (After Nina Bagley)

We are gatherers
The ones who pick up the broken bones
From the sticks and stones
And words.
And old souls, fallen by the wayside
Of life.
Hollows that look like eyes once alive,
Shells of people, not whole, but lovely
In their brokenness.
We are the ones who bring home
Empty souls
and place them in a safer place
To keep for what? For how long?
It matters not.
What matters is the seeing, the gathering,
Lives filled with
Remnants of love and life,
The traces of hope, a lingering
ghost of a laugh
That might come from the
Shell.

The Ache

The wind knows how I feel
tonight,
pushing against doors
firmly shut.

Whispering desires
to those who
slumber.

Evening Debates

Am I a fool to do what I do?
Enthusiasm and exhaustion run high.
Sleep slams against the walls of intellect:
I crave the crashing waves of life,
But they
Overwhelm
 me
    too.

Can one
S u c k   the marrow out of life
In their
Sleep?
Is this
Why we are
Called to Dream?

Oh rest! My weary head adores you!
Oh world. Let me bid you
Adieu,

At least until
Tomorrow.

Shadows

The night was nothing more than shadow
yet the terror felt so real.
Are we afraid of shadows?
Can they consume
and digest and
spew us forth
with the intensity that this darkness
screams is possible?

Yet the earth keeps turning—
the mercy of God insists it is so—
night turns into day
the day dawns
the shadows shrink.

Lift my face to the rising sun!

Break from this volcanic cloud
whose substance is little more than illusion,
who cannot bear the presence of the Holy One.

The light has come into the darkness
and the darkness WILL NOT overcome.

The Beautiful Storm

Joy drips from the broken
skies:
the steely grey
cracked open by
the bow.

Heralds trump as
sparkling soldiers play:

crash and waltz in a world that shouldn't be.

The chaos and the beauty
sweep the earth,
the storm refreshes with her
purple light.
Pungent and delicious is the air;
freshness buzzes with
infused delight.

For Pauline & Mel.

Single Mum Guilt

The sauce is wrong
The noodles are wrong
That's not the shop I wanted to go to.
Why do I have to share?
This is MINE, it's not fair.
I'm hungry, get me water now!
Why should I get the bag?
You make me SO MAD.
I want to live with dad,
least it's fun over there.
Don't wanna clean my teeth,
Mouth is sore, it's giving grief…
Hey, look! Mum, can I have that lolly
PLEEEEEEEASE??!!

Then I yell,
And they cry,
And I wish I could die,
Cause life's so hard—
    so freaking hard—

yet I try and I try.

With my head in my hands
I think— *is this who I am?*
Am I good? Am I bad?
I wasn't good enough for dad...

So I must conclude that
the good girls always lose,

But then, perhaps you can't be good if
you're a slut.

I Wish I Were a Puppy

I wish I were a puppy,
I'd have all the love desired.
People would adore me, give me everything required.
I'd be scolded with a smile
When I messed up on the floor:
They'd never leave me
permanently ushered out the door.
I wish I were a puppy:
They're allowed to give affection
In overwhelming buckets-worth
Without fear of rejection.
Their drive to please and cuddle
Doesn't get them labelled needy:
(People seek them simply for these qualities indeed-y!)

But I am not a puppy,
I'm a broken human being
Fear and love leak out of me
And leave me here unseen.
I'm tired of the trying, the surrender, the rejection,
The carrot of forgiveness
Guaranteeing no protection.

I wish I were a puppy,
Alas I'm only human!
I'll travel down this human road
And try to have some wisdom
In decisions and relationships
Of which I am no master…

If only I were a puppy
Maybe life would be less harsh-er.

The Drifter

A leaf blows ragged on the wind.
Floating on the flurry, being tossed and turned
And twisted sideways.
Strong, yet brittle,
Battle-bruised and bowed:
High and mighty living
Stripped by nature's forces
Forcing downward.
Lie.
Lie upon the earth.
The bones of rotting dreams
Painting dainty lacework corpses
On the ground.
How can things so pretty
Die a quiet death upon the dirty floor?
Is there ever more?
Or do we drift upon the ragged wind
Until the force of nature strips us bare?

And we are left…

Monuments of broken dreams…

earth after rain

nothing stops me in my tracks like the smell of
earth after rain
crickets creaking
the pause of pungent air abuzz with clarity:

    Hope is the smell of earth after rain.

rising from the roads
cleansed and earthy
clean yet dirty
fresh and birth-y
awash with the beauty and mess of new life.

Time Goes Dripping By

Time goes dripping by,
Syrupy and sluggish:
Drop by drop.

As our days reduce
to the lives beneath our nose
do we smell the burn
of sadness
or the sweetness
of relief?

Can we breathe in deep
and snuggle
into this golden glow?
An amber moment
drop into this gift
we didn't know
we needed.

Yet here it is.
Here it is.
Here it is, my sweet.
Cry if you must,
mourn the loss
of things left
incomplete.

But time goes dripping by
my loves,
Time goes dripping by:
Syrupy & sluggish,
Golden & delicious,
Moody & contentious…

But precious, above all.

Messy and Bright

In the still and
The small
My heart feels
Full.
Chaos toned down to
Only that which
Really counts.
The joy outweighs
Frustrated tears
Frustrating weary souls…
Because the soul
Need not be weary
On this day.
Find rest with the
Babe in the straw—
The smell of dung
Cannot outweigh the
Glory.
This is my story.
His story.
The Messy
And
The Bright.

Part Two: The Eye of the Storm

I have never experienced a cyclone. However, as a kid growing up in the era of natural disaster blockbuster films, I was fascinated with the idea of volcanoes and storm-chasers. Watching the heroes entering storms to save the day, quickened my spirit. Reading classics like *Frankenstein*, where the protagonist has epiphanies in the presence of wild storms and desolate terrain, thrilled me. Becoming a storm-chaser was high on my bucket list.

The introduction to life-storms took some of that wind from my sails. But I am still awed by strong displays of power, whether in nature, or human nature.

The Bureau of Meteorology (2023) describes a cyclone as a giant, dangerous, rotating cluster of thunderstorms, producing extreme winds, rainfall, and damage. Their violence pushes outwards in a rotating manner, surprisingly often leaving the centre of the mega-monster with a clear and calm outlook for a period. This is known as the eye of the storm. On their website, The Bureau of Meteorology warns, "it is important to remember when the eye of a cyclone passes over a location, there will be a temporary lull in the wind, but that this will soon be replaced by destructive winds from another direction." When amid a storm, even one of notable violence, there are moments of reprieve. Sometimes, it becomes so calm you can see blue skies again, for a time. While in the eye, it is important to do two things. Firstly, take a breath. Inhale deeply and take stock. Secondly, recognise that the storm is not yet over. When in the eye of a storm, you are still right in the midst of it. You might find that your circumstances are still impossible. But here is grace: being given a chance to breathe, within the impossible. There is still a need to brace for further violence and heartache before the storm passes. But in moments of reprieve, take the opportunity to recoup, and find new strength.

Daughter of Eve

"It was this woman you gave me…"
"I was tricked, and I ate..."
"There will be pain in childbirth, paradise you did forsake."
And now we walk among thistles,
And flesh and blood hurt
And I feel unclean,
Like I know I am dirt
I can feel it underneath my skin.

Am I really still a daughter of the King?

Brain Fog

When the heaviness comes
My heart sinks inside
I know it won't last
But in the meantime

I can't help but curl up
To push through the fog

As the colours are drained and
the   boundaries   are
                              lost   . .
             .

Broken

Broken life,
Broken heart,
Broken soul.
This is the journey I have known.
Once I knew the
Secret to Contentment.
Now I'm lost and lonely and offended.
Well I know what I don't want to be,
But does it matter when I'm drowning out at sea?
Clinging to the wreckage of my days,
Attracted to the roaring of the waves.
"Sleep, sleep," coos the siren song,
It matters little if I'm right or wrong.
No matter if I thrash or scream
No matter if I wake or dream,
This is the journey I have known.

The Herald

When the days are getting bitter
The depression out of hand
And the words they scald like liquid ice
That carves a reprimand
On a soul already broken
On the shattered plains of life
And your sodden soul it wonders
If it's had enough of strife…

Let the wonder of your soul
Soak up the life of shattered plains
Brought back into communion by
The sodden soaking rains
Break the soil, carve a path
Glacial in scale
Hand the land's depressions
Seed to bite into the meal of
The lengthening of days:
It just might be this winter's eve
Has ushered in Spring's Praise.

Remember This Moment

Remember this moment.
May it be
Lived:
Every second, every minute.
May it be
Seen:
Each other, all the hurts, and fears, and beauty.
The only
Time
Is NOW.
Make your home here,
And here let your heart rest.
If some tears spill over,
That's ok.
They are part of the moment too.
Remember to Breathe.
The breath of life is
Also in this moment.

Remember it.

Jeff (Until We Meet Again)

This morning I woke up to death.
It draped its veil over my day.
Not a veil of hazy excitement— a new life
awaiting the aisle's end…
 but the end of a life awaiting…

       Tears?
       Celebration?

No.

Awaiting an extended fare-well.

The grief is not for him—
not when I KNOW he is
rejoicing with the angels,
   -   living in the body of his youth,

jamming with the
                Heavenly Band of Hosts.

No.

The grief is for the l   o   n   g   good-
bye,
knowing the earthly parties will have to wait until the angels
can join us in dancing.

      For now, tears will have to be our partner,
      the wake a remembrance-meal in lieu of
the Last Supper
      we never had…

My dear friend.
Walking this earth with you was Such
an honour.

Your time dancing around this sun has been replaced
by Eternity with The Son.

Save a dance for me.

      …Until we meet again.

Balloon

I see you.
Bright and full of the
breath of life.
Made to mark celebration and joy.
Lifted high, buoyant, and light.

But people don't see when you've been
stretched too far,
filled with hot air and pomp
Until your insides squeeze you
And you want to scream
But the wheeze you exhale leaves you flabby,
misshapen, lifeless
Exhausted
And sad.

The thing is
You were made
To hallmark the
Good times
And outshine the bad.
So lie on the floor.
Allow the loose insanity to
rest
 Until He fills you up
Again.

For Katy.

The Machine

we have handed our control
to a faceless
monster.
it doesn't know
and doesn't care
but　turn,

turn,

turns
spitting out what doesn't fit
promoting what doesn't work
and working to the bone
those fit for promotion.
when we prostitute
our lives to Policies and Procedures
instead of protecting
our people and places
a monster is born.

                  its monotonous turning
                        turns up the heat
                        turns out the good
                    trumps up the tyrants
           and while the people cry out

       it turn,

                turn,

                        turns.

For the teachers and nurses

Do Not Get Drunk

Do not get drunk
On regrets
And old scars
Mistakes
Past hurts
Nostalgia
Replacing
One burn
For another
An empty vessel
Fuelling the fire
Of an empty heart.

Dark on dark
The canvas of a broken heart.

The funnel focusses fiery tears
Bottled behind a headache
Of heartache
Locked in clenched teeth
and an
upward chin…
Screaming to be released
And washed away.

An amber tide

Staves off the tsunami
Of surrender
Overwhelming
The Whole World
Until everything is dark.

Dark on dark.
The canvas of a broken heart.

Do not get drunk
On fears
And strong feelings
Rejections
Reflections
Offences
The stars in the night
Can only shine bright
When the sky is cleared
Of both cloud and light
When we can't study
Imperfection.
God in the dark.
Paint upon this broken heart.

For Ed

Hell, there is nothing wrong with you!

Your crazy is not your own,
Merely an unwelcome cloak weighing you down
While they all "look" like they're doing fine.
Wonder, and struggle, but don't be confused:
You are NOT alone.
Scream, gasp for air,
Just remember to breathe.
While I am here,
I will help you make it back up.
I know you are scared,
And the depths are very deep,
But don't sink:
Reach out, we will hold you up,
Shine a torch into the darkness
Of your mind.
If the switch turns off,
It can turn on again.
And you can eat
And sleep
Laugh and talk
Once more.

I Am His Moon

Born to reflect Him
          in the darkness

    —in the dark, to show His

              likeness—

Born to create waves and commotion.

          Born to sway the ocean.

A Poem for a Mother on Her Birthday.

Strong and unwavering,
her love branches out,
embracing all.
Stretching in praise towards her maker,
welcoming all in the shade of her protection,
a safe landing place for us little birds,
seeking wisdom,
seeking shelter,
seeking care.
She is warmth,
radiating love, compassion,
Teaching me the wisdom of the seasons:
Commit to rest.
Burst forth in the glory of new growth.
Take time to let the old weight drop away.
Rejoice in your abundance.

Always willing,
Always loyal,
Always caring.

A majestic oak,
Planted by the Lord,
Displaying His splendour.

I am your little wren.
And you:
You are my
safe landing place.

For Trish.

Mall Thoughts

While tired and seeking a moment,
With a Subway and a drink,
A blind man moseyed past me at the mall tonight.
I stopped:
It got me thinking
"I wonder what he sees?"
Can he see the muddied music
Misting lonely from the ceiling?
Does he taste the conversations peppered across the floor?
Is the tang of clinking crockery enticing to the soul?
Does he laugh at me for believing the wood-veneered chair who called out,
"Take a seat! Have a rest! You deserve to relax in this COVID-safe space with its cheerful big-green-propaganda-ticked stickers!"

I squirm on the seat, not as comfy as promised:
Muscles and bones all weary from living,
Yawning into this cavernous void.
The man clacks past with his rolling stick,
And I think,
At least he gets to miss that garish game that continues to yell at me,
"IT'S TIME 2 WIN! Blink. Blink. Wink. Wink. YELL!"
Enough contemplation.
My Subway dinner has had time to work its magic.
It picks me up, and together, we head home.

In the Moment

What a gift to be present!

To hear happy chatter twirl in the air,

A biscuit smooth and crumbly in my hand:

Contentment of a week that is at its end.

Winds of Change

Come to me on the breeze
and billow into my soul
the winds of change,
adventure,
and to know I'm not alone.
Expand in me a freshness
where the sorrows cannot root.
Reignite the colours
that were fading in the gloom.

Blow me down!
Blow me Down
Blow me clean away!

And I'll B R E A T H E
                              clean air…
Enliven me, this day.

Pink Bedsheets

Today I bought pink bedsheets
Quite the oddity for me:
The wild girl without the
Patience for such primp-ery

They lay beneath my covers—
      The ones adorned with pastel flowers –

Setting off my chiffon drapes
And accenting the showers
Of the little crystal droplets
Sparkling from my chandelier

And I wonder when this softness
got permission to appear?

The wild girl still loves the touch
Of dirt and grubby road
But somewhere space was made
for more than fighting traits alone.

She made peace with loving beauty,
She made space for holding still,
She found out you can have joy
Even if on depression pills.

Part Three: Coming Out of the Storm

There is nothing quite like the smell of earth after a storm. No matter how severe the rain, when the sun breaks through the clouds, and everyone comes out of hiding, there is a holiness in the atmosphere. There is an inevitable sense of hope and expectation. Wonder. Refreshment.

In my experience, there is no other phenomenon that produces such an effect. And it is my favourite feeling in the world.

In this life, people are cruel. People are also amazing and compassionate. And we are both those people. Some storms, we cause for other people. Others happen to us. We all need justice *and* mercy.

Which leads me to wonder: Must we go through the storms in order to soak in the holy? Is it the preceding tearing and the stress which makes the air so pure and sweet afterwards? Are storms given to us to teach us greater compassion? I do not know. All I know is that storms are inevitable. And the aftermath, while often devastating, also brings great beauty. So, if, in this world, I must endure the storms *in order to* experience the grace...then I shall.

The Thing I Admire Most

The thing I admire most
Is not exemplary behaviour,
Or people who are whole,
Or stand tall,
Or never fall.

No.
I admire
                GUTS.

Those who fall
But
                        Up.
            Getting
    Keep

Those who Know
They are not

The Bees Knees

But live on their knees
Because of that Knowledge.
Those who repent
Seven times a day
Are my heroes.

The broken whole
Who struggle to stand tall,
And often fall.

I don't need the

Once-Were Rebels
Who have Never Fallen Since.

The pedestalled perfectionists
Proclaiming High Priest status,
"Protecting" us from the

Prince of Peace…

I want the Man who used
Prostitutes and Pirates
to change the world

Who knew the frustration
Of fellowship,
And loved
Completely

Anyway.

When did we replace Him

with Performance?

The thing I admire most
Is not a Thing…

But a Him.

Warrior

I am a wanderer in a foreign land, thrown
into an unusual war,
yet made to be a
Warrior.
Arise, arise,
yes, take your stand,
albeit in this foreign land.
Stand tall, stand tall,
with head held high,
with spirit sword
and shield nigh.
We shall fight
and we shall win
for our gracious
Mighty King.
Arise, stand tall
that we may
be
the warriors
standing tall and
free.

Prayer of a Broken Vessel

Break me Jesus.
Squeeze the bitter juice of
broken life from my body,
and replace it with zest:
Zest for You, for life,
for loving.
This body is so fragile.
I feel less than clay –
closer to soggy mud
slipping down the slopes
as the rains relentlessly
ravage this dirty soul.
But this is not Who I Am –
Certainly not to you.
You made me on PURPOSE
and my purpose is Your Brightness,
shining out loud,
to prove Your glory.
Fossick me for your flecks of gold.
Uncover the gold nuggets
hidden in this muddy soul
and prove Your worth.

Love Allows the Journey.

Love allows the journey,
Gives space to not understand.
Love accepts the messy,
Enters the dirty places to help us out.
Love washes feet. Hands. Hearts.
Without throwing dirt or accusations.
Love walks quietly through the sorrows,
Without letting go.

Love allows the journey.

Freedom Dance

Another day for joy
to dance with grief.
A two-step life discordant
with the beat
      of my heart.

Another day to dance.
To cry? To scream?
To dream. To sing…

But mostly:
To LIVE.
To LOVE.
To BREATHE.

Indeed,
the freedom to exist
in Him.

A Weekend Blessing

may your days be Delicious and Joyful
may you relish the Kiss of the Sun
may the Blue Sky enhance
the Colours of your Soul –
give you space to Breathe Deep and Have Fun!

A Closer Look

Look Closer.
The beauty is right there.
Look Closer.
Beneath the putrid air.
Beneath hysteria,
Beneath the "I don't care".
Look Closer.
Within the Deep Despair,
When things are So Unfair,
Beneath that Angry Glare,
It's There.
A Caress of Pure Breeze,
A chance for you to Breathe,
A glance of "LOVE ME, PLEASE!"
It's There.
The tiny pricks of light
That pierce the darkest night,
The hugs that help to right
What has been wronged.
A Moment to unwind,
A "You've been on my mind"
The extra hands when words need to be shed.

A perfect little flower,
The beauty of a tower,
The awe of storming power:
It's There.
Look Closer.
He whispers when
The world just wants to Yell.
Look Closer.
Take the hand that leads you
Out of Hell.
Let Heaven be your Guide,
As you navigate the Mire.
Look Closer:
The beauty is
Right There.

For Emily.

The Wings of Forgiveness

The wings of forgiveness
are not formed in beauty,
freedom or light
but in claustrophobic darkness
so dark
it disembodies
Completely
until one cannot
remember what one WAS,
as the building blocks of a life once lived
melt into oblivion,
drained of all recognition,
       and time…

until a tiny tinge of light
cues a struggle as large
as life itself,
a forward force unstoppable
towards an impossible future,

until suddenly…

There are crumpled wings!

Then coloured wings!

Then strength!

Then… impossibly…

Flight!

She Shall

And she shall live
many lives and lies
and cry and shy
away from it all
but in the end like a moth
to flame she will burst alight
and do it all again
this phoenix of beauty and
Repair.

After glow

The   sun
     heavy
and stillness of the soul
      hang
        quiet
in the evening air.
Bodies, content and sated from
l o n g   d a y s
of No Import,
Lie comfy in the tired silence:
the consequence of
                Life Lived
                    Beautifully,
for a
      s u s p e n d e d
                    time.

Happy?

I am not happy with my life.
How could something so transient
Possibly
Describe
The intricately sorrowful beauty
Of waterfalls
Crashing
With majesty and mayhem
Against rocky daggers
Dangerous and glorious,
With wild winds
Cascading into
Tempests of passion or hopelessness,
Ecstasy, excitement, expectation
Or pain?
Happiness doesn't capture quiet pools of contemplation
Dragged from depression through
Gravity or granite caves until it
Hits the Light and curls up in reprieve.

No.

I am not happy with my life.
It is far too precious for such a cheap label.

Home

What a strange feeling
After all these years of drifting
I feel like I'm home
In a half-life between
Clarity and chaos,
Strife and surrender,
Discord and daydreams.

Life.
What a strange experience
Of stumbling and strengthening,
Wondering and worshipping,
Comforting and crying.

And I wonder, have I lived before I'll die?
But I realise,
This
Is
Living
And in this surrender,
I
Am
Home.
You.
You were right that
You CAN fly

And you SHOULD fear.
But
Not exactly like you thought.
Angels and air vents are not the enemy,
And flight looks different than you thought.

Twenty-three houses and counting…
You are yet to experience
Two.
The darkness you suspect
Has not come near –
Two Decades to relax before those
C r a c k s
Appear.

And though you SHOULD fear…
Don't.
And because you CAN fly…
Do.
And eventually, I promise,
You'll find

Home.

Gift-Wrapped

Our hearts are gift-wrapped
with bandages,
tenderly holding the bruises and wounds
that once unwrapped
have become precious
lessons of courage
for others to share:
on proud display
as the scars speak stories
of how
we overcame.

God's Poem

I am God's poem,
A masterpiece of mayhem and majesty:
Like confetti, I'm scattered, but sparkly!
Made to display marvel and melody.

Meticulously manicured – imperfections celebrated,
He has lined me with stanzas of beauty and heartbreak
And weaved me in words of wonder…

Despite the occasional
SPLAT!
I am a beautiful ballad.
Sometimes a limping limerick,
Often too over-emphatic –
Yet a perfect couplet complete with rhyme,
A well-spaced verse
writ
in well-spaced time
And nothing, if not linguistic!
I'm whole, and I'm not.
There is gold in my shatter.
SMASH! His Glory shines.

…I am God's Poem.

And He is Mine.

Rest

Rest
Is not a dirty word,
Though it is a hard one.
It is hard to
Be still
Long enough to let
The dirt dry and flake
From your
Weary soul.
It is hard to
Unstrap the fetters of the world
And place them at God's feet,
Where we were never supposed to pick them up
But did.
Rest requires surrender
Of the control we
Never

Really

Had.

To accept the roll of that
Massive wave looming.
In order to find the Deep places
Beyond.
To still long enough to hear
The selah in the psalm.
To HEAR it,
And to listen
And to KNOW.
Be Still.
Be STILL.

Be still.

God
peace
hope
life is waiting there for you.

Acknowledgements

It takes a village to raise a baby. The following people have been my village for this project. I am beyond grateful for you all. Firstly, to Sofia, Raf, and Igor, my three brilliant children. None of this would mean anything without you guys. To mum and dad, for trusting me with this personal investment. I know my ideas are often wild. Thank you for agreeing that this one wasn't "completely ridiculous". To the world's Greatest Aunt. Aunty Gaye, you have believed in me since day one. Your unconditional love is inspiring. When I grow up, I want to be you. To Rosanna, Luke and girls: you lot define true friendship and family. Your support has meant the world to me. To Jess, who has walked and prayed with me even from afar. Thank you for your faithfulness. To poet David Tensen, for taking me under your wing in Poetry Chapel Volume Two and showing me how to navigate the world of self-publishing. I hope I've made you proud. Also, for introducing me to the lovely Rachel Huckel! Rachel, your editing and website building prowess have been awesome. Your belief in this project has inspired me to keep reaching towards the prize. To Margo, for believing in me before I did. And for being my beta reader – what a huge blessing! To Bitty and Lucky at Pure Laser, for being my sounding boards and cheerleaders through all the excitement and drama. To my Facebook family. You guys have given me support and encouragement and kept me alive and moving forward more than you will ever know. I love you all deeply. To all those who have believed in me even through my mess and abrasiveness. Thank you. Lastly, to Matt Tommey and team. You guys changed my life. Thank you for being obedient to God and the Spirit. I am proud to be one of your Army of Artists. And to Ed.

References

Australian Government - Bureau of Meteorology (2023). *Tropical Cyclone Knowledge Centre.* Available at: http://www.bom.gov.au/cyclone/tropical-cyclone-knowledge centre/understanding/tc-info/ (Accessed: 21 May 2023).

Delffs, D. (2019). *The Faith of Queen Elizabeth: The Poise, Grace and Quiet Strength Behind the Crown.* Zondervan.

Oxford English Dictionary. *Life.* Available at: https://www.oed.com/ (Accessed: 7 March 2023).

Prince Harry, The Duke of Sussex. (2023). *Spare.* Bantam UK.

Roberts, H. (2022, 19th September). The Queen through the decades from the 1920s to the 2020s. *Berkshire Live.*

https://www.getreading.co.uk/news/reading-berkshire-news/gallery/queen-through-decades-1920s-2020s-22219117 (10/05/2023).

Shelley, M. (2009). *Frankenstein.* Camberwell, Victoria: Penguin Books.

life: or something like it
also available in eBook format.

Also featuring Catherine Sharpe-Lewis:

Winters Never Last
From winter's grief to summer's joy.
A poetry collection for all seasons.
By David Tensen and Friends 2022

w: www.catherinesharpe-lewis.com
e: hello@catherinesharpe-lewis.com

About the Author

Catherine Sharpe-Lewis has been telling stories her whole life. Growing up in the country, and coming from a literary family, she had two dreams as a five-year-old: to be a farmer, and to write. She became a teacher, instead. Catherine still writes and dreams prolifically, and intends to write many and varied poems, books, and stories for the world to enjoy. She has spent her adult life not fitting into the mainstream and coming to terms with this disparity. When she is rich and famous, her plan is to live on a functional communal mini-farm, complete with community garden, repair café and a shipping container house. And chickens. Lots of chickens.

This is her first solo publication.

www.ingramcontent.com/pod-product-compliance
Lightning Source LLC
Chambersburg PA
CBHW020328010526
44107CB00054B/2018